Telekinesis

How to Become a Telekinesis Master

(A Guide to Moving Objects and Psychic Energy Manipulation for Beginners)

Thomas Pena

Published By **Tyson Maxwell**

Thomas Pena

All Rights Reserved

Telekinesis: How to Become a Telekinesis Master (A Guide to Moving Objects and Psychic Energy Manipulation for Beginners)

ISBN 978-1-7750277-3-7

No part of this guidebook shall be reproduced in any form without permission in writing from the publisher except in the case of brief quotations embodied in critical articles or reviews.

Legal & Disclaimer

The information contained in this book is not designed to replace or take the place of any form of medicine or professional medical advice. The information in this book has been provided for educational & entertainment purposes only.

The information contained in this book has been compiled from sources deemed reliable, and it is accurate to the best of the Author's knowledge; however, the Author cannot guarantee its accuracy and validity and cannot be held liable for any errors or omissions. Changes are periodically made to this book. You must consult your doctor or get professional medical advice before using any of the suggested remedies, techniques, or information in this book.

Upon using the information contained in this book, you agree to hold harmless the Author from and against any damages, costs, and expenses, including any legal fees potentially resulting from the application of any of the information provided by this guide. This disclaimer applies to any damages or injury caused by the use and application, whether directly or indirectly, of any advice or information presented, whether for breach of contract, tort, negligence, personal injury, criminal intent, or under any other cause of action.

You agree to accept all risks of using the information presented inside this book. You need to consult a professional medical practitioner in order to ensure you are both able and healthy enough to participate in this program.

Table Of Contents

Chapter 1: Meditation 1

Chapter 2: The Ethics Of Seducing Others With Your Mind 16

Chapter 3: Knowing Versus Doing 27

Chapter 4: Mental Seduction Works 41

Chapter 5: Telepathy & Mind Control 53

Chapter 6: The Science Behind Telekinesis 67

Chapter 7: Visualization And Intention Setting 76

Chapter 8: Practicing Telekinetic Exercises 83

Chapter 9: Sharing Personal Experiences And Success Stories 101

Chapter 1: Meditation

Relaxation: (For mediators looking to boost their influence over what the general public currently has, this method is vital). Use this strategy first regardless of whether I explicitly mention it in every section.

Any distracting thoughts are reduced through this practice. The meditation eliminates distracting external as well as external influences. It's simple and extremely important. The chances of success are slim in power meditations if cannot be in control of your thoughts. The base of all exercises is this. It isn't easy to regulate the way your thoughts are interpreted However, persist. There will be great tranquility and joy once you've completed your mental silence.

Utilize the Quiet-Mind meditation for the beginning of your meditation. It is more important to pay attention at your own heart.

Then, you can settle into an elongated position, and point your eyes at the object that is in front of your. Keep your eyes on the external object. Focus your attention on that space. Then, hold your breath in a steady manner. Be sure to slowly however, you must keep the breath in a rhythmic manner.

Focus your eyes, and close them. your eyes to the black screen. Be aware of the world around you. Work to put all thoughts away until nothing but silence and peace remains. Stay all the time that you can.

This may seem extremely simple. It's possible that you are thinking "How could this give me power?" I'm here to assure that this is only the start. It's just the beginning of a stage in.

My personal experience using this practice is the following: As I sat in a place that was public at night when I was unable to focus my mind, I calmed it. The lights in the facility began blinking after I had reached the state of a calm consciousness and started breathing into a state of vitality (you can find out more information about this in the next chapter). The next thing I knew I was able to hear thoughts from others experiencing their thoughts, their feelings, as well as seeing their physical manifestations. In a few further minutes, I opened my eyes. The universe seemed to be pixilated since I began to recognize its actual form, which is nothing but a pulsating light.

My attention was then shifted to focusing my focus on a pile of garbage that was nearby. Within a split second an instant, a white and opaque mass of energy burst from my forehead and struck the bag. It then exploded in a loud way. Also, I began to see red ball of energy floating in the vicinity of my home. (See the following page ...)

For more information about the energy field to better understand the Aetheric Plane, and the best way you can explore these. I highly recommend that purchase this book:

The Mentalists Handbook_ An Explorer's Guide to Astral, Spirit, and Psychic Worlds HERE

Going Deeper Meditation and Breathing Energy

It is crucial when you meditate to take the time not just to quiet your mind, but to as well bring your mind to an euphoric state. Your mind functions in four main levels along with some sub-levels between. These sub-levels are not considered because they are not important to the exercise.

The four stages of the mind include Beta (awake), Alpha (relaxed), Theta (deeply at ease; nearly sleepy) as well as Delta (fully sleepy). Once your mind is at the Alpha stage, it is possible to focus on meditation significantly more effectively. Theta is also a possibility however it requires time to keep your mind focused without falling into Delta. For a transition to Alpha and then Theta when you've improved in your skills, perform this exercise.

Step 1: It is crucial to perform the meditation in a location in which you won't be scared. Perform the Quiet Mind Meditation (Q-MM).

Step 2: "Feel" yourself stepping down a step into a dark place or descending an elevator. If you're using the escalator approach, make sure that you're looking the opposite direction in your mind to get the feeling of being in reverse.

Step 3: Once you're ready to go, you can feel your body falling backwards to a more tense stage. If you've performed this right, you'll be in a state of trance and then you're fully prepared for start working.

It is important to remember that the key to this practice is not creating an elaborate strategy, but instead using the easy, but very effective way of reducing the brain's state of mind. Benefits of this meditation apart from enhancing your spiritual abilities, also include enhanced senses, body relaxation as well as lower blood pressure. relaxation and a calm mind.

If you observe anything or experience anything unexpectedly during this process Don't be afraid. If your mind is at peace you are more likely to be willing to be open to new experiences including seeing energy beings, hearing voices from the astral plane and experiencing bizarre feelings.

Breathing Energy

The topic of energy can be very wide . But, it's essential that you understand the basic principles of energy through breathing; else your meditations won't have "kick "...so to speak. At the moment, it is best to breath in energy using the following method.

Step One: Perform the Q-MM and the Going Deeper Meditation (GDM). Step 2: Take a deep breath through your nose. Then breathe out your mouth using your lips to create that form a hollow. You will feel a distinct sensation in your body. The experience will differ for every person.

Imagine your body as covered in golden-white illumination. Step 3: Feel the feeling that is happening.

You don't need to think of the force. However, you must experience it to allow the technique to be effective.

MIND CONTROL | SEDUCTION

The Mini manual explains the elusive method of seducing someone else by using your brain. When you adhere to the guidelines in a clear and consistent manner These techniques will let you in on an undiscovered world within you and allow you to take a look at how your mind is able to influence other people.

Human beings as adults are well-versed in the concept of the mind's manifestation. If you say it this way "mind manifestation" it can bring to your brain images of the 'bizarre', magical or paranormal and so on. The mind is capable of manifesting things directly through human thoughts. However, if you examine every day and you'll see many examples of human beings' capacity to create 'stuff' through thoughts.

Everything human-made that surround you began with the minds of a single person or a group of individuals. Imagination plays a key role. The concept or idea is initially conceived within the brain. It is then discussed by oneself or with others.

The mental process continues to draw a finished idea within mind(s). mind(s). This leads into physical process aspects that initiate the process of manifestation. If the goal is creation of a brand new device, blueprints diagrams are begin the physical process, from which manifestation would continue until the birth of the device. Processes for developing physical components are also underway. In the end, the gadget will be produced, using machines or humans in order to bring that initial mind-generated concept into the real world. Even how you arrange your furniture is an example of thought-to-manifestation, whereby your plans/ideas are first created in the mind then you do the physical process (like pushing the couch) to completely manifest your intended re-decorating idea (thought).

We're well-versed about the idea of mind manifestation or mind manifestation. We already have a good grasp in this field.

The physical objects surrounding you is not an example of things that are obvious or unnecessary. All of them are examples of thought/mentality manifestation. Once you look at your mind's abilities from this perspective and begin to recognize that you're already advanced in your mind's capabilities already. In a subliminal basis, your mind functions as an advanced device: For a mere few...it is a storage device for information, it processes data, enables the communication with your spoken language, and regulates the bodily activities (advanced mechanisms in and of their own) and without the conscious mind being required to complete the task. Remember these points before you venture into the realm of mind power, for it is true that you're not even a novice. Your mind truly is amazing and can make physical objects from one idea (idea). Your inner mindset (belief) that provides the magical substance that will ultimately allow you to access even greater powers of the mind and the manifestation of your mind.

SEDUCTION

In this article, I'll describe the concept of 'mind seduction' for other people' as having the capacity to sexually or erotically entice an individual using just the power of your own mind. If you employ these strategies to someone else, they is bound to them over time, and with strong feelings about sexual. Usually, it is a sign of "falling in love"

It begins to happen on the person you want to impress. Communication with the individual will be required. The person does not have to be one that you have met. But, eventually communication will take place and it to provide useful feedback on the impact of your actions in influencing others.

The strategies presented in this article have proven to be effective absolutely. It's instantaneous and it will take some lag that will take a while before you notice outcomes. Automatic and instant sexual influence is a skill in the mind which takes the time. Similar to any other skill it is important to master the ability through consistent and effective training. Keep your mind and body tranquility instead of a hurrying mentality. It will manifest. When your skills improve the speed of manifestation increases. If you're unfamiliar with these strategies and techniques, you can expect anything between two weeks up to several months to see results observed. The results are directly affected by how long you are involved in the process for at the very least in these "early" phases.

The patience and the tranquil (that internal smile) will pay off it is when you start to observe the effects of your actions becoming visible at a physical level. the person you influence will be so attracted to you, that they'll want to spend time there with you.

Chapter 2: The Ethics Of Seducing Others With Your Mind

SEDUCING OTHERS WITH YOUR MIND

Seducing other people by using your imagination could be a topic that is controversial. Being the sole individual who is in charge of your destiny It is up to you to determine whether or not to employ these techniques on an person. I am not in a position to determine your ethical standards and values.

The details in this article will be provided to the reader to help them understand to gain knowledge. Some people are reluctant to implement the strategies for themselves, however they'd want to understand about them and the ways they can influence someone else. Some people are interested in knowing methods to attempt and avoid being influenced by someone who could influence their behavior.

However, if one wants to discuss the morality in this area of mind lure, then there's a variety of topics that could be discussed Ethics of manipulating an individual against their wishes. Ethics of influence over those who are married or in different relationship. Ethics in influencing the young. Ethics of the amount of influence an individual can have. Ethics regarding the publication of such information and the implications that could arise beyond it. It is also a question of whether or not it could be a smear on the negative factors. While the techniques are designed towards both women and men however, in many cases the question of "trying to influence women' is brought into the spotlight. The subject of our personal capacity to think and create as opposed to God's creative power can be a topic of discussion. I am a big advocate of debate and discussion in order to assist everyone understand their own life as well as the environment around them. Be aware of the potent effects of these strategies. Take care as they perform and yield interesting results.

FIND YOUR TARGET

"Target" shouldn't be taken as a 'victim. It is your objective or your purpose. To reach your intention,

It is important to first determine whom you would like to influence. The majority of people have their eyes on a person already.

A person they would like to spend time with. That could be the person they want to focus. Other people can venture out and discover a new person.

There is no requirement to have any prior or recent contacts with your potential person of interest. You could have a relationship with someone whom you've never had a conversation. It's best, especially in the beginning phases, to have an individual you regularly see.

As someone you know from work or in your life. As you advance with this technique it is not necessary to need to live within the same town to be your goal. Begin by locating an individual close to you, someone whom you see frequently in order to gather information. The ability to watch your subject during the time that you influence them gives the opportunity to gain valuable feedback. Feedback can be a valuable tool that will not only help you advance by enhancing your skills in brain power however, it also assists in steering you to the correct direction if you're engaged in a undertaking. Keep in mind that you're not just using your brain to influence the thoughts and emotions of someone else as well as to alter situations and events; all of that is done in order of achieving your initial intention. The process of monitoring your goal (gaining feedback) helps you better evaluate a situation, or track the course of an event or series of happenings. Through careful observation and planning it is possible how to use your influence to the best way or the frequency with which you practice.

After you've found the target you are looking for, have a notebook that is thin or something like that for keeping track of everything you have observed. Notes are a useful instrument that will improve your general mind-control and level.

WHAT WILL HAPPEN TO THEM

If you decide to have an impact on someone else, an variety of events will occur. A few of them can be observed (and ought to be recorded) but others may not be evident. Different people react in response to the seduction effect. People are more easily attracted, and others are resistant. However, all reactions indicate one thing that is certain the target is extremely, incredibly attracted by you. It will be a deep feeling and powerful, and will be similar to feelings of 'fallen in love.

There is no time when the individual feel pressured or controlled. Although the emotions may seem overwhelming (which is typical) or conflicting (which is uncommon) but the person who is being targeted is likely to feel that they is beginning to attract towards you.

In the end, your target may contact you and begin to communicate with you in a more regular manner. It is recommended not to engage in any kind of flirting initially with the person you wish to influence. Concentrate on being nice and humorous (making people smile or happy) and let your influence to bring about the change.

Most of the time, targets create walls in the event that they suspect they are being targeted by someone seeking to get them. Keep it simple, and your actions are causing them to be more enthralled by them. Be cautious in the event that you notice a indication that they are experiencing an erotic attraction to them. Give it time, and let the subconscious mind of the individual to be able to feel happy for you. While you're doing this, you're informing their subconscious mind by the intention of your choice.

YOUR DAILY ROUTINE

Then you will start your day-to-day routine. These are the methods you'll be using to put into an effort to reach your aim of using mental tricks to seduce one. Set aside one hour every daily. It must be the first thing you do. The time is divided into two sessions to control your mind: So you'll be performing one half-hour session in the day and an additional session later at the same moment in the day. If necessary, shorten the duration of each session by 15 minutes. However, it is preferred to schedule one hour-long sessions. The most serious mind control enthusiasts could even have the urge to hold more sessions, possibly up to two hours each every day. Noting down your experiences is recommended.

INNER VISION

The method of seduction involves certain visualization techniques. The thoughts of your mind have the capability to alter your environment creating change in the physical realm. If you can see an object in your imagination (via visualisation, imagination or other methods.) provided it's performed in a steady relaxed, steady, and consistent manner...it begins to alter the air around you and can have a significant impact on those around you and events within your lives. It's a huge subject that is discussed in Mind Control Manual. Mind Control Manual and will not be addressed in this piece.

CALMING THE MIND

It is essential that your session commences with a relaxing in your thoughts. That is it is essential to feel relaxed and comfortable position to enjoy your sessions. When your mind is relaxed and your brainwaves become more relaxed, they decrease in frequency. They then get more in tune with the naturally occurring frequency that the earth experiences (7.85 cycle per second) which allows for an interaction between your mind as well as the environment around you. The mind is relaxed, which allows you to see more clearly while bodily processes can be reduced to a minimum.

I'll leave it for you to decide the most effective method to enter an unwinding state. To help beginners there is no need to be concerned or obsessed with how comfortable your body and mind are. Simply allow a relaxed state to happen and your meditation will perform. In time, you will be able to learn to enter more relaxed states. It is best when you keep using the QMM/GDM meditation.

Chapter 3: Knowing Versus Doing

Many times, novices worry or concentrate on things like how comfortable to feel and whether their visions are crystal clear. One of the most important things to keep in mind is that practice brings ability, and it is what will improve as time passes. It is not necessary to be concerned about the clarity of mind or specific relaxation techniques, rather you should concentrate on practicing the actual visualization methods on a regular basis. This will allow the degree to increase naturally with the course of. If one does not think this way it is easy to be absorbed in the technicalities of theory or data instead of actually utilizing the precise visualization strategies. A lot of people who embark in a spiritual journey are entangled among the myriad of knowledge available and do not spend enough time working on the personal implementation of the religious principles they're studying. It is possible to spend a long time in the library, reading books, and informing yourself about facts knowledge, theories, and other information. But you realize you don't spend any time experimenting with your own ideas and taking action. That's why very many people fail to reach the highest amount of personal power even though they have read every publication on the subject.

If you're able to relax your body and starting your session take a step back and don't fret if you're relaxed enough, or if you're executing right. Simply do your work and your skills and techniques will develop and improve as time passes.

Knowledge VERSUS doing Often people worry about or concentrate on questions like how comfortable they are as well as whether their visions are crystal clear. Most important to keep in mind is that as you practice, comes proficiency, which will grow with time. You should not be concerned about concentration or exact techniques for relaxation, instead the focus should be on practicing the actual visualization strategies on a regular basis. This will allow the improvement to naturally happen over the course of. If one does not think this way you can be absorbed in details or theories, instead of actually utilizing the precise visualization strategies. Many times, those embarking on spiritual pursuits can get caught up in the plethora of available information and do not spend enough time in the actual practice of the principles they're studying. There is no limit to the amount of time you spend in the library, reading books, and armed with information theories, information, and theory. But you realize you don't spend a lot of time conducting personal experiments and taking action. It is the reason that very many people fail to reach the highest amount of personal power while they might have the most comprehensive publication on the subject.

When you are settling your mind before beginning your session, don't fret whether you're relaxed enough or are practicing the techniques correctly. Do the work, and your skill level and technique will develop and improve as time passes.

INFLUENCING YOUR TARGET

The half-hour session you have scheduled must include these two kinds of visualisation. A period of 20 minutes is recommended to touch erotically (in your brain) the person you are talking to. The final 10 minutes must be spent constructing scenarios. Let's go into more details.

In order to simplify Visualization can be seen just as an act of imagining, or as when you're thinking about it. You can simply allow yourself to think. If you are able to visualize things through your imagination is not vital. The ability to visualize becomes clearer by practicing.

In the initial 20 minutes, you must imagine that you touch the person with a sexual or erotic manner. Concentrate more on the sensation as a whole and the effects it has upon the other person rather than the setting or the scene you're within.

OK? Make sure your touch is gentle and non-erotic, but not and hostile. Your brain's eye (imagination) pay attention to the sensation of touching, instead of imagining yourself making contact with. To practice touching (touching) objects in your head, visualize yourself being able to feel cotton balls or touching your pen, or rubbing some stones. Relax and take your time with the objects you imagine in your head and feel the firmness or gentleness. These practice sessions differ from the seduction sessions.

To erotically touch someone is a matter of prior experience or knowledge of sexual intimate relationships. If you've had previous sexual encounters, you are already able to come up with ways to kiss somebody. If you've never had experience before, you can use your imagination to the best extent you are able to. The erotic touch and the caresses must be targeted at common erogenous parts that the person you are targeting is like the nipples or the genital regions along with other soft places of the body like the stomach or facial area. When you make contact with the person inside your mind, try to you should feel (as as best you can) what reaction that the other person will feel for example, the sensation of wetness (if the person you are targeting is a female) or a feeling of hardness (if the person you are targeting is a male). The goal is to slowly make contact with the individual and sense their response growing within your head, ultimately sending them into the point of asexual coma. Make sure to take your time and do not be rushed over your touches. Try to cover every sensual part of their bodies. There are many areas that could be explored over several sessions. The feel of your target being 'turned on' because of the mental touch will be prominently displayed in the visualizations. In the final 10-minutes of the 45 minute time should involve picturing both of you within situations. If you want to create a sense of love in your subject, think of (visualize) both you with your partner being together,

Cuddling with hands, holding hands on the sofa and so on. Choose one thing you can focus on and focus for the whole 10 minutes.

When you are in these sub-sessions of scenario Try to bring as many emotions and feelings as you can. It is possible to see the goal,

Be close to the target, hear their voice, feel the surrounding area of your location, etc. What is most crucial to imagine scenarios is feeling "now. The goal is to be able to see the scene through your mind as though you were at the moment. It's not later, it's not then...but today.

For that additional dose of faith into your procedure, while you're conducting your session, be sure to keep yourself in a state of smile...an inside feeling of knowing that the efforts you put into it will be rewarded.

If you are uneasy, make it appear as if you are. This will be your perception. This feeling comes from the confidence in oneself and an unbreakable confidence that your mind's power is powerful and effective. In that feeling of confidence it also encourages patience,

The sense of seriousness and calm...whic they are all feelings (energy) that operate along with your visualisation sessions (thoughts) to ultimately manipulate and alter the surroundings (e.g. the way you make events happen). Another topic that can be further discussed within the MCM.

The description below describes the 30 minute period you have to complete. 20 minutes of thinking touching and sexually touching someone as well as their intense arousal/reaction the touch. Ten minutes of scenario situations.

The entire session must be performed twice daily at least. Do not rush and take your time. the time, and don't get eager to observe the results right away. Although a response outwardly is a few weeks away and you don't waste all of your time doing your daily exercises. In fact you're training yourself to be more mentally prepared and you're educating yourself to develop patience (which is confidence that the your desires will be fulfilled as they are commanded by you) You are constantly assessing the influence over the other.

THEIR PERCEPTION

Your influence is having an effect on the intended target. The images (thought orders) penetrate deeply into the subconscious of your target. Then they begin to feel erotic, or love emotions toward the person you are. The victim will usually try not to reveal the feelings...just because you're not sharing your feelings while you live the day to day life of other people. In time, however, you'll be able to see the indicators.

It is your goal to make them be thinking about the person you. They will soon be able to develop erotic thoughts toward your. They'll find themselves ever more attracted by your. If they're alone they might feel that they are drawn to dream about you, particularly when you've had a few hours of sessions with their behalf. It is likely that they will occasionally fantasize about you, too when they are asleep.

MONITORING

It is the reason why keeping a watchful eye of other people's actions is essential. Note down in your notebook meticulous notes on their actions about you, no matter how insignificant it might seem. Even if you're not communicating with the person you are targeting, just be aware of them whenever you encounter them. If you are talking to or have a connection with the person you are targeting, be sure to watch for signals when talking with them. Keep in mind what was discussed earlier. If you're communicating with a person you want to talk to, make yourself available with a warm and pleasant (perhaps humorous) manner...not with a flirtatious or a game-like manner. If someone else feels that you're trying to be flirty with them...then emotions for them could go up. It's the kind of wall that you need to knock by using your brain ability. Engaging with the subject by engaging in conversation with them is a great method to get past walls. You should act as if have a great and secure acquaintance or friend as you create the best path to thinking communication.

Chapter 4: Mental Seduction Works

Keep to the method you have chosen take notes on your work and intended target's reaction. This person is now motivated to get close to you without doubt. This will occur.

TIPS ON MIND CONTROL

Be confident about your capabilities and appreciate the process of learning and improve these abilities. The key is to try new things, but don't get too far towards your own techniques until you've seen consistent positive results using the strategies described on this page. Be consistent with your training. If you practice daily in a year's time, your skills will be at an undoubtedly higher standard. Do not let up on your goal. If you decide to choose to pursue a different goal it is possible to work with the one you previously worked on simultaneously (extra time). Make sure to consider what the ethical implications of this issue are prior to launching into techniques to control your mind. If you are aiming for positive outcomes and non-harmful, you'll be okay. If you want to utilize the power of your will to harm or cause harm to anyone else and cause harm to others, then you're the proud recipient of the negative force that will try to steer you on a darker, more dangerous direction.

You shouldn't reveal to the person that whom you're attempting to influence, due to obvious motives. Do not reveal to anyone that you're employing methods to influence other people (others are likely to doubt your motives and hinder your work).

THE WORLD OF MIND CONTROL

Mind control, also known as your capability to create and influence your desires into reality it is a broad subject. The article here is brief in its explanations, but it contains enough details for anyone who is looking for the ability to seduce an individual with the power of mind. The subject can be delved deep. The unique aspect of developing your brain power is the ability to personalize your methods. Your mind is unique to anyone else. That means that you'll eventually come up with your own strategies by experimenting and experience. The process of visualization is what that initiates and creates the process of manifestation. The methods of visualization can be as innovative and distinctive to you as the individual that you are. The ability to influence others by your imagination and imagining scenarios with these methods isn't a technique that was invented by one or another. It's likely been practised and experimented with throughout the ages by those who seek the higher art, and has been reported on in one form or the other. Mind control is a popular issue right now due to the focus regarding 'what they're doing to us' e.g. the government's mind control. You can influence others and we can be controlled by others. The person who hones the ability to master can be the person who has become proficient at controlling other people and who is adept at not being subdued. The field of mind control is broad and it can become very sophisticated. As an example, the use of psychotronics and radionics ('thought machine') combined with sexual psychological influence can be a potent combination. Mind power may also be used to enter into different areas of practice, such as lucid dreaming (controlling your sleep during the midnight) and off-body travel (your awareness of your body and traveling to any place) remote viewing and many more.

TELEPATHY & Advancing methods of harnessing the mind's power

TELEPATHY & MIND CONTROL|

Are you curious about what mind reading is, or how mind control work or what it takes to improve it? This kind of question is frequently within our minds. This article will provide strategies to increase your mind's power.

Many people aren't convinced of the reality of these powers or when they come across such abilities, they tend to deny it or declare it coincidence because of their level of unbelief.

A lot of us have had the experience psychic contact. It was as if you were considering someone else, then they call you. The person wanting to get in touch with you, sent you an enthralling message, and you were able to recognize it through your thought channels.

The mind is far more powerful abilities than we recognize. However, we've been confined in the limitations of our third(3) dimension of thinking as well as our logic. As we grew into a young person, we were taught that the thoughts we had and our experience of the supernatural are just fantasies, and that we needed to not be thinking about it. Our imagination is placed in the confines of our physical reality that the limits of our imagination. This impacted our belief and our perception, and over moment do those memories fade away or a mere idea that is difficult to track back.

In this book, the powers of the mind will be exposed and you'll get back the abilities you lost.

The power of mind

Imagine the images of your mind along with all thoughts and your imagination as the climax in Etheric Vision that is connected to all mind, matter as well as future events. Every thought is psychokinetic (PK Psychokinesis) conductors of energy. People, objects or situations are interconnected. This explains the law behind attraction, as well as the laws of manifestation and synchronicity predictions, and more. It is possible to manipulate psychokinesis by imposing psychokinesis through deliberate thoughts about things, people, events or situations. All things that exist in this world as well as the universe contain in the form of energy, and they are linked by the mind. Every thing in the universe as well as the universe are manipulated through psychokinesis, which is a deliberate thought process. The psychic predictions are a different form of psychokinesis. The thoughts of psychokinesis that are forcefully induced can affect your surroundings and people such as your personal life events as well as global things.

Psychokinesis is the apex of any paraspychololgy-related issue, the mind reader, telepathy manifestations, mind control remote viewing astral projection, reading of auras and many other things.

"When you think of a person in your mind then their mind becomes your mind, the longer you hold an image or images of them in your mind the longer you have access to their mind, will, and future, this also holds true for objects, people, situations, and events".

Anonymous

The methods in this list are endless. You can come up with your own with your imagination. You can come up with anything and create something nobody thought we would accomplish. Get creative. Your creativity of your mind will generate endless concepts. Around the globe police officers, law Enforcement Organizations, Military, Large companies, friends, neighbours and boyfriends, mothers as well as fathers that you may not have a clue about, utilize these strategies to get you, and on each other constantly without being aware of it. Turn your back to tell them to tell the truth. Then, they will give them a lie, when they inquire about why and then explain to them why they aren't required to view the thoughts of your eyes. After that, you force them to look at a horrifying image. Then, they will make their tears so they can see the issue.

Mind Control Techniques

(EYES) Aggressive Mind Control

Take a look at someone with their eyes, hold your eyes and imagine images or thoughts and it is now possible to transfer your thoughts through their eyes. Whether they know or not. This process is known as Nerual Langustic Programming; or NLP. It is also known as optikinesis. As long as you are holding your mental image in their minds, the more strongly you're attracting the mind of that person to this picture. This is basically making them read the thoughts of your brain.

Take a look at someone through their eyes. Mentally in your mind, imagine them crying. they'll want to begin crying. They'll be tempted to cry and begin to feel unhappy.

When you look them in their eyes. Imagine that they're angry and throwing things around or hitting you. And they may feel the desire to carry out the act if they do doing something about it. The emotional power of this is powerful over an individual. Imagine someone doing anything in front of your eyes. Not only did you create the emotion, you also generated that idea, as well as it is their intention to act accordingly.

(EYES) Passive Mind Control

Mind control through the eyes means that they are the act of holding a mental image or image in the eyes for only a brief period of time instead of for a lengthy duration, consider it as a covert.

Chapter 5: Telepathy & Mind Control

(EYES) Passive Mind Reading

Lo look at people's eyes when they are conversing. Your thoughts are neutralized so you do not be thinking. Take a look at their eyes and your thoughts will enter yours If you just leave your thoughts empty. It can take time to master to perfect this, however when you've got the time and know how to perform it, you will also achieve this.

ADVICE: If someone is aware of how to read minds using eyes, they'll always advise that you should look them through their eyes and tell they have some thing. When you make someone Mind Forced to look at your thoughts, they will be able to perceive your thoughts (Read Your Mind) subliminally by looking at them with eyes, essentially turning you a mind reader with the eyes. They don't know that they are thinking their thoughts.

District Attorneys, Police officers Judges, Doctors, spouses, girlfriends, wives generally will through this with you. They won't be able to tell that you that they read your thoughts with their eyes until they instruct them to check their eyes. ....don't try it.

(EYES) Aggressive Mind Reading

Keep their eyes on the screen and force a picture or image that relates to the topic you would like to have their mind flash forward. If, for instance, you suspect that your partner was watching nake girl images on the web, then your girlfriend could subliminally show naked images of girls in her boyfriend's eyes. He will then look through the most recent memories of naked women in his

Computers or phone calls.

Imagine mentally a picture of the ISIS flag, while gazing into the eyes of a U.S. soldier's eyes and it will instantly reveal previous thoughts that they have stored in their minds. This may be triggering PTSD within them. It is can be a type that is a form of NLP Control of the Mind. Control.

(MIND) Aggressive Mind Control

By using a mental image of someone in your head could lead someone to give in to your wishes. Visualize that person as joyful and smiling They will not only be able to see smiling and happy thoughts within their minds, but they'll also feel joyful and begin laughing. The longer you keep the image in your mind, the greater likely it is to have an impact create on them.

If you are looking at a person imagine them getting angry, throwing things around, and getting into anger

Then they'll begin to feel your thoughts, then act the way you expected that they would if they couldn't manage them.

Imagine that they give you a hug, and if you do this correctly, you will receive a hug, but a there are certain relationships that must be established prior to time under certain situations.

If you're currently dating, and whatever you think you imagine them doing, continue to on doing it and apply it with a lot of force. The mind's seduction can be quite real.

(MIND) Passive Mind Control

Just thinking of someone short is a type of mind control passively. If you imagine somebody right before the phone is answered and you realize it was the person that you imagined, in no way knew they controlled your mind the person you thought of and thus they appeared inside your brain.

When you think about someone, they'll see you in their head as well. Whenever they are thinking about you, they will be able to see you within your head. Thinking about and remembering someone can result in inadvertent control of your mind and mind reading by both sides.

(MIND) Aggressive Mind Reading

Similar to an aggressive mind reading through the eyes, and also Mind Control Aggressive simultaneously. It is important to imagine their actions with mind control so that you can see the next thoughts that pop up within your head concerning the subject. Example: A chef at the kitchen would like to find out if the food preppers are eating their foods they're making. Chefs will imagine food preppers eating the food they are making, and the food prepper can only see the idea as a memory or an additional thought and whatever thoughts the food prepper was experiencing will be seen by the chef. The longer you cling to an image, image or even a face and face, the more thoughts you are able to see. If you hold it for long enough, the person will be aware that you're within their minds if you have a brain reader. It is important to keep your distance from those who have mastered these techniques. If you don't understand these techniques, then they're like a puppet that is tied to strings and you're the puppet master. Mind reading using your mind is also possible in a distant location, and time are no longer an issue and it's an instant move.

(MIND) Passive Mind Reading

Mind reading passively is a the ability to read the mind of a person. Utilize mental visualization to determine the things you wish to observe about someone else and what your brain will tell you.

(BODY) Aggressive Mind Control

You are able to physically hit or smack, pull or even touch someone through your mind and body without touching them. You must use your entire mind as well as your body for this to be accomplished, the more powerful your feelings are the more effective. This is similar to the scene in the subway on the film Ghost when the man moves the container. The guy is using all the resources it takes through his passion. It's like you're planning to touch your target and then you can feel it in your hands and visualize the image in your head. It's an extremely powerful strategy and its effects are extraordinary. Anyone you're applying this technique to will be thinking and experience the sensation. The ability to read minds can be achieved with this technique too.

Visualize your thoughts using your mind, and then use your body until you reach the point where you physically experience the person.

Touching a person just like you do in the physique, however you do it by making use of your body and mind and the person will feel it.

It is possible to be someone's ghost by using this trick If you decide to apply this technique to the extent that you want. Try something new with this.

(BODY) Passive Mind Control

Utilizing a reference line that is from Project Switchplate on the CIA website, this site explains the in depth process of psychokinesis. Utilize a clear and simple visualisation of the individual in your mind that is doing something, and then you can be able to control the action of that person, it's is as easy. It's totally secret and those you're performing this for will not be aware that you are making the actions. It can be done by looking them in the eye, or even through a mental image.

(BODY) Aggressive Mind Reading

Mind force them to read the words employing the body techniques described previously. Like mind reading eyes and the mind when you are in a combative mode, you will be making use of your body for this. It is easy to tell how a person reacts by clearing their mind to keep it in a state of clarity before putting your body on them and you can clearly observe the reaction of their body and experience them.

(BODY) Passive Mind Reading

The idea is that you are seeing your mind and then feeling within your body the things they want to say to you.

Locations

Create mental images of an area you would like to visit and the more you hold the image or image, and then focus your brain like a camera lens you'll be able to be able to clearly visualize in your mind the location you wish to observe.

People

Make use of mental images to visualize the character you would like to be able to visualize. As long as you keep an image of them in your mind, and focus your attention as if you were imagining a camera, the more photos you receive regarding the person. You must make use of discernment your memory and thinking. It is possible to force into a particular location and observe what pictures you receive back. If you believe or think that they're at home you can remotely view their home and see if there are any pictures of them to pop in your head.

objects When you use visual imagery to imagine things, your mental imagery tend to take you to other memories, places, people or current happenings all the time.

Remote Event

Make use of mental imagery within your head to achieve an outcome you want anyplace in the world. It could be called an intention or a prayer practice, the more ideas you think about it and the more you let your emotions spill let out, then it'll be realized. Do not stop contemplating it till the moment arrives, and it'll happen.

X-Ray Vision (Etheric Vision)

Etheric Vision refers to anything that you are able to see using your brain, and that implies that you are able to make use of Etheric Visual XRays using only your eyes and mind. Only one percent of the globe's populace is able to perform it right now. However, with some practice, you can increase that percentage up to all of the world's people. The way to accomplish it. ...... Consider the person or object then clear your mind.

Visualize in your head what images you're getting back. Be focused on the subject you're looking at and then focus your attention and focus to view the things you wish to perceive. Etheric Vision is using your third eye, in combination with your eyes. The effect is that you are seeing through the two eyes with the third eye. Also, you can observe your subject and let your mind discern what is from the other end. Theric visions allow you to see the field of auras for a person and allows you to observe the thoughts of a person while looking at the body, and also observe their body to any reason. It requires a sharp mind in order to achieve this, however through practice and patience, it is possible to achieve this.

Chapter 6: The Science Behind Telekinesis

The science behind Telekinesis is the study of the relationship between our mind as well as physical objects. Although telekinesis is often dismissed as just a myth or a trick, there's research-based evidence to suggest otherwise. Scientists have devoted significant effort in disproving the myths of the phenomenon and investigating its nature.

The most important aspect to understand telekinesis is to understand the role played by the brain in the process. It has been proven that specific brain regions, including the prefrontal cortex as well as the parietal cortex, get stimulated when performing telekinesis. It is believed that the brain plays an important role in initiating and directing the telekinetic action.

Additionally, knowing the fundamental physics of telekinesis is vital. Telekinesis is usually linked to the principles of quantum mechanics that define the behavior of particles on a microscopically small scale. Certain theories suggest that telekinesis can be explained through manipulation of quantum fields or making use of quantum entanglement.

The impact of consciousness on Telekinesis is an additional fascinating field of inquiry. There is a belief that telekinesis may be an example of the power of consciousness in humans to affect physically-based phenomena. There are many questions regarding the possibilities of using telekinesis to improve areas like engineering, medicine and even the space industry.

But, studying the science of telekinesis presents many difficulties and limits. These phenomena can be subtle and hard to recreate within controlled environments. In addition, the significance of intention and belief in telekinesis can complicate the research procedure, since skeptics claim that subconscious biases could influence the findings.

Despite the challenges The potential for telekinesis research is promising. With our knowledge of brain function and quantum mechanics improves and we are in a position to discover the secrets of telekinesis, and discover the full potential of it. By doing this we could also learn more about the connections between telekinesis as well as other psychic phenomena. This will further expand our understanding of the human mind as well as its incredible abilities.

Developing a Strong Mind-Body Connection

For a healthy body-mind connection, concentrate on living a balanced life style and participating in exercises that boost both mental and physical well-being. When you incorporate mindfulness techniques and techniques for healing your mind to your everyday routine to increase your abilities to utilize the potential of Telekinesis.

Here are some strategies to build a stronger connect between the body and mind:

Physical Fitness:

Engage regularly in exercise like yoga, tai-chi and Pilates for improved the flexibility, strength and stability. These types of activities do not just promote health and fitness, they can also assist to calm the mind as well as increase awareness of the body.

Practice deep breathing exercises in order to relax your body and ease tension. This is possible via activities such as meditation, or even simple breathing exercises.

Mental Well-being:

Engage in activities that challenge your mind for example, solving puzzles, reading or learning new skills. It helps keep your mind active and alert improving your mental wellbeing overall.

Try mindfulness meditation that is, focusing your mind to the present moment, without any judgment. It helps you become more aware of yourself, decreases anxiety and increases the body-mind connection.

When you incorporate these exercises to your daily routine you will be able to build a stronger connect between your body and mind, which is crucial for unleashing the potential of Telekinesis. Be mindful of your own limitations and engage in these exercises with a relaxed mind.

The body and the mind are connected By fostering the connection between them, you will be able to unlock your full potential and tap into the amazing potential of telekinesis.

Meditation Techniques for Enhancing Telekinetic Abilities

Integrating meditation in your routine will help you develop the ability to telekinesis. Techniques for mental concentration can be crucial in building your connection with the body and mind, as well as unleashing the full power of Telekinesis.

By meditative practice, you will help your mind focus and focus, both of these are vital skills to controlling objects using your mind.

An effective method for meditation to increasing telekinetic ability is to do breath exercises. Through slow, deeply breathing, you are able to relax your mind and draw your attention back to the current moment. This will improve your concentration and mental clarity which allows you to channel your energies towards the telekinesis.

A different technique that is beneficial is to align your chakras for Telekinesis. Chakras function as energy centers within the body. Aligning them will aid in circulation of the energy needed to control telekinetics. Begin by visualizing every chakra starting at the bottom of your spine before moving towards the top on your head. Pay attention to each chakra and imagine that it is spinning and radiating bright energy. This process aids in the balancing of your energy field, and helps to create an enlightened connection between your body and mind.

While practicing meditation It is important to stay open-minded and try diverse methods. Try different techniques that include guided visualization and affirmations or meditation on mindfulness to determine which one works best for your needs. Be conscientious and patient when you practice, since building telekinetic capabilities takes time and effort.

Integrating meditation into your daily routine will greatly increase the telekinetic capabilities of your body. Through enhancing your concentration techniques and balancing your chakras you'll be more prepared to tap into the potential of your mind to control things.

Chapter 7: Visualization And Intention Setting

Discover the benefits of visualization and establish clear goals to improve your telekinetic capabilities. The use of visualization techniques is powerful tools to tap the potential of Telekinesis. Through creating vivid mental pictures of your desired result it is possible to train your brain to link with the force needed for moving objects using your mind.

To improve your telekinetic capabilities with visualization, consider the following methods:

Create a mental model prior to moving something, picture the object in your head. Take note of every single detail including its size and color, through its weight and texture. Imagine you are being in contact with the object, sensing the energy that flows throughout you while you are preparing to take it to the next level.

Make a habit of daily affirmations: The affirmations you make are statements of confidence that strengthen your faith of your telekinetic skills. Make affirmations like "I'm capable of moving things with my thoughts' and 'I possess the ability to direct the flow of matter', to prepare your mind's subconscious to be successful.

Utilize guided imagery: Guided imagery involves listening audio recordings which guide the user through a visualisation exercise. They usually feature soothing music, as well as voices encouraging you to envision certain scenarios, like being able to move objects easily or bend spoons in your head. With continuous repetition, guided imagery will improve your ability to visualize and improve your telekinetic skills.

Clear intentions are essential when it comes down to the process of telekinesis. When you clearly state your goals it provides an unambiguous direction for your energy and mind to follow. In setting your intentions It is essential to remain specific, focused and optimistic. As an example rather than saying "I'd like to move this object', you should say, 'I'm going to move the object effortlessly by using my brain. This clearness of purpose helps you bring your focus and energy in line with your mind, making it more likely that you will succeed in action that is telekinetic.

As a result, techniques for visualization and setting clear objectives can be powerful ways to increase the telekinetic capabilities of your. Incorporating these methods in your routines, you'll be able to improve your connection between mind and body, and unleash the full power of your telekinetic abilities. Be open to new ideas be consistent in your practice, and observe as your skills increase with every visualization and goal you make.

Strengthening Psychic Energy

The development of your psychic energy is vital to enhancing the ability to communicate to and affect your surroundings. Channeling and healing energy can be powerful tools to boost your psychic power and maximize your abilities.

Psychological healing involves the act which uses your psychic skills to treat yourself as well as others. This involves tapping into universal energy, and then directing it toward the person that is suffering. To increase the strength of your psychic energy for healing, it's crucial to begin by developing a awareness of compassion and empathy. It will enable the person to be connected with others in a deeper way and send healing energy toward the people around you. Do a practice of meditation in order to calm your mind, and then open to the energy that you receive and then transmit. Picture yourself being surrounded by the bright healing light. Imagine that this light is flowing across you, and then into the person who you are helping.

It is also a great method of boosting your psychic power. It is the process of allowing universal energy to flow through you, and applying it in order to achieve particular goals or tasks. In order to increase your capacity to channel energy, begin with a meditation or visualisation. Think of roots emerging beyond your feet and into the Earth and connecting you with the energy of it. Imagine an enlightened white light coming into the top of your head, and then flowing throughout your body. If you can channel the energy, you'll become more tuned to the flow and will eventually be capable of directing it to certain goals.

The development of your psychic power is essential to unleash your psychic abilities. When you engage in healing psychically and channeling your energy that you channel, you will increase your connections to the world around you and gain the power of thought over the physical world. Make sure you approach these activities with a clear mind and by consistent, regular practice you'll unlock your complete psychic abilities.

Chapter 8: Practicing Telekinetic Exercises

An effective method to enhance the telekinetic capabilities of your body is consistently completing various exercises. Telekinetic visualization is an effective method that will help improve your mind-matter connection. Through visualizing the movement of objects through your brain by visualizing them, you're training your brain to be convinced of the existence of telekinesis. This turns increases your capability to regulate the physical world.

For the first time, to begin experimenting with telekinetic visualization Find a calm and relaxing space in which it is possible to focus on your work without interruptions. Begin by picturing a tiny object, such as pencils, within your head. Imagine the pencil floating the air in front of you, and imagine yourself applying gentle pressure in order to make it move. Visualize the pencil responding to the mental instructions you give it by shifting and rotating in the manner you want you want it to.

When you're practicing as you continue to practice, increase the difficulty of the objects that you imagine. Then, you can move on to bigger objects like an object like a chair or book. Try manipulating the objects using your imagination by visualizing them moving up, spinning, or moving in the air. The more vivid and precise your vision, the better your control of telekinetics will be.

To master telekinetic control, you must have perseverance and commitment. It is crucial to perform these techniques regularly, and ideally at least 15 minutes per daily. In time, you'll see improvements in your capacity to imagine and manipulate objects using your mind. Make sure you approach these activities with a positive attitude and trust in the potential of Telekinesis. If you keep practicing you can unleash the full potential of your mind's capabilities.

Using Tools and Objects for Telekinesis Training

Utilizing tools and other objects could help you develop your telekinetic capabilities. Implementing objects, props and even instruments into the telekinesis program can help increase the concentration of your brain and increase your connection between body and mind. Three ways that to use equipment and objects to enhance your telekinetic abilities:

Visualization aids for visualizing: Making use of things like crystals, candles or art work can act as focal points for your visuals during the telekinesis exercise. Focusing your thoughts upon these things will help you increase the concentration of your mind and increase your abilities to alter your energy. The act of imagining the motion of these objects in your brain can assist you to enhance your telekinetic capabilities.

Dowsing rods and pendulums They are employed in training for telekinesis for practicing controlling movement. Utilizing a pendulum or dowsing rod, one are able to control the energy surrounding you and steer it toward the you want to achieve. Begin by focusing your thoughts to the object. Gradually expand your intent to move the object.

Utilizing technology plays a major role in the training of telekinesis. There are devices and apps accessible that measure and monitor your brainwaves and help you monitor your progress and develop your skills. Virtual reality also allows you to create a virtual space where you can test your the telekinetic movement and interact with other objects.

Utilizing objects, props as well as instruments during your telekinesis classes can offer the opportunity to focus training and improve the overall learning experience. Explore different methods and see what resonates with your most. Keep in mind that telekinesis is an art that takes dedication, perseverance and a receptive mind. If you are dedicated and have the right equipment, you will be able to unlock the power of the mind over things.

Harnessing Emotions for Telekinetic Power

For you to fully realize your potential, make use of your emotional power and let them enhance your telekinetic capabilities. They are an incredibly powerful power that can be harnessed to boost your telekinetic capabilities. If you can manage emotion in a targeted and controlled way and you are able to greatly enhance your abilities to telekinesis.

Utilizing your emotions to create telekinetic energy requires an knowledge of your emotions. It is crucial to stay conscious of your feelings and the way they impact your life. If you are aware of and accepting your emotions, you are able to start to direct their energies towards your goals in telekinetics. The emotions of enthusiasm, anger, and determination can be extremely powerful to boost your telekinetic skills.

For you to be able to control your feelings, it's essential to achieve a peaceful and focused state of mind. The practice of mindfulness and meditation are a great way to achieve the state that allows you to feel connected with your emotions at an even deeper scale. Through observing your emotions and not relying on judgement, you will be able to manage and channel the energy of your emotions towards physical and mental activities.

It's equally important to keep a positive and optimistic mindset while using your emotions to gain the power of telekinetics. Fear, for instance, or doubt could restrict your growth and the abilities you have. If you cultivate a positive outlook and believing in your personal abilities, you will be able to unlock the full potential of your thoughts.

Engaging with emotions is an important part of releasing your telekinetic talents. When you channel your emotions, and channeling them towards your goals in telekinetics and goals, you will be able to tap the full power of your abilities. Keep your mind focussed, calm and optimistic, and you'll be able to see the amazing power your emotions unleash.

Overcoming Doubt and Believing in Your Abilities

Believe in yourself and your abilities is vital to conquer doubts and unlocking your true potential. In the quest to unlock the power of telekinetics, doubt could be among the most significant obstacles against your progress. By gaining confidence and embracing the abilities and abilities, you will be able to conquer these doubts and unlock the endless potential that your mind has.

To conquer self-doubt, is crucial to realize that doubt is an inevitable element of learning. All people experience doubt and fear whenever they try something new or demanding.

What's important is to not allow these fears to define you or limit your progress. Instead, make them motivation to go further and show yourself you're capable of accomplishing incredible things.

The first step to build confidence is creating realistic goals, and then taking small wins throughout the process. Every achievement, no matter the size of it, will increase your confidence and strengthen confidence in your capabilities. Be surrounded by a positive crowd of fellow-minded people that believe in the potential of your character. Their support and encouragement will give you the confidence it is important to persevere.

Another way to conquer doubt in yourself is to do some visualization.

Imagine yourself using your abilities of telekinetics and imagine the positive effect it will be able to have on your own life and those around you. This practice will allow you to build confidence that you are capable and will eliminate any doubts that remain.

Take the time to embrace your strengths. Accept that you are blessed with unique talents and possibility of making a positive impact within the world. If you are able to embrace your talents and taking them on and expressing them, you'll create an attitude of confidence that inspires others, and increase your confidence in your own abilities.

Believing in yourself and building confidence is the first step to unlock the full potential of your mind. If you believe in your capabilities and taking them on board will help you beat any doubts that be arising and harness the endless potential of your mind.

Protection of Your Energy and Avoiding negative influences Protecting your energy as well as avoiding influences that can negatively affect you is essential to maintain your positive attitude and increasing your capabilities. When you are navigating the realm of telekinesis it's crucial to define and preserve boundaries for your energy.

Being conscious of the energy surrounding you and choosing to interact with people who encourage and help you grow. With clearly defined boundaries, it is possible to keep the negativity that others emit to drain your energy and hampering your growth.

A great way to safeguard your power is by using positive affirmations. The power of affirmations is that they can help to rewire your mind to create a positive mental state. Through repeating affirmations, such as "I'm strong and resilient and able to have positive energy it is possible to counter the negative forces that attempt to penetrate your mind. It strengthens the belief that you are capable and protects your mind from negative external influences.

Alongside affirmations, it's crucial to pay attention to your surroundings and the people which you live in. Influences that are negative can take on many forms. They include unhealthy relationships, negative mindsets as well as environments that are brimming of negativity. If you are conscious about spending your time with supportive, positive people and soaking yourself in positive environments and environments, you build a layer that blocks the negative influence.

Be aware that preserving your mental and physical health is an ongoing procedure. This requires self-awareness, self-care and the dedication to maintaining an optimistic mindset. Through setting boundaries for yourself and including positive affirmations in your everyday routine, you will be able to protect your motivation and create an atmosphere that encourages you to grow and progress in telekinesis, and beyond.

Interacting with others in the Telekinesis Community

Joining forces with other members of the community of telekinesis can be the necessary support and motivation on the way to your goal. Belonging to a group that has the same goals and interests is extremely helpful in improving your telekinetic skills. When you practice telekinesis in an environment with other people and learning from each other and gain an insight about different approaches and techniques which can enhance your capabilities. There are five ways that getting involved with the telekinesis world can benefit your practice:

"Share experiences": Connecting with people in the community of telekinesis allows you to share your experiences as well as learn from those who have developed their telekinetic skills. The exchange of information can assist you in understanding how to improve your abilities and also what isn't save you time and energy in the practice you are currently doing.

Motivation and motivation: Telekinesis training can be difficult and even frustrating. Being as part of a larger community may help you find the motivation and motivation to persevere. If you witness others achieve successes, it motivates you to persevere and aim to achieve your own personal breakthroughs.

Learning new techniques experienced practitioners within the world of telekinesis usually employ their own distinctive methods and strategies.

Through their connections to discover and master these diverse strategies, building your own range of skills and possibly finding methods which resonate with you.

Collaborative practice: Group exercises allow you to work with other people to develop your telekinetic skills. Working together you will be able to learn from one another's strengths as well as limitations, give guidance and encouragement to each other, and together expand the possibilities of what you are able to achieve.

Connections with friends: Interacting to other people in the community of telekinesis can result in lasting relationships. It's a great way to meet people who are similar to you in their interest and are able to appreciate the difficulties and pleasures in pursuing Telekinesis. Friendships with these people can create solid support while you grow and discover your talents.

Joining the community of telekinesis can bring many benefits to your experience. From sharing your experiences to discovering new methods to gaining ways to boost your motivation and build friendships Being part of an online community will help you improve the telekinetic capabilities of your body and make the journey satisfying and enjoyable.

Chapter 9: Sharing Personal Experiences And Success Stories

Personal experiences and triumph experiences can motivate and inspire people in the community of telekinesis. When people talk about their experience to harness the power of their mind over the physical world It not only shows the personal progress they have made, but can serve as a symbol of hope for those who are following an identical journey. Stories like these provide a sense of encouragement and validation to people who are in doubt or struggling with their ability.

The most intriguing features of telekinesis is the ability to bring about a deep spiritual awakening. By utilizing telekinesis it is common for people to find themselves getting deeper into their awareness and becoming more aware of the interconnectedness between everything. The spiritual development can be an experience that is transformative, since it opens new realms of possibility and new perspectives.

If you are sharing your own experiences when sharing personal experiences, you must be able to approach the subject with an open mind and an analytical outlook. While some might think that the reason for their success is purely rational explanations from science, others might discover a deeper metaphysical or spiritual reason. It's important to appreciate and appreciate the many different views and perspectives that exist within the telekinesis world.

Through sharing their personal stories as well as success stories, they are not just inspiring others, they help to increase the wisdom and knowledge of the phenomenon of telekinesis. Each tale offers a distinct perspective, and sheds light on the various methods, difficulties or innovations. Sharing experiences creates an atmosphere of camaraderie and helps to facilitate the growth and advancement of the practice of telekinesis overall.

sharing personal stories and successes stories within the telekinesis community can be a valuable method for personal growth as well as spiritual awakening. This can inspire and encourage others as well as contributing to the overall knowledge and understanding of this amazing phenomenon. Don't be afraid to tell your story and shine a illumination for those who are on the journey to harness the power of your mind over the physical.

Exploring the Ethical Implications of Telekinesis

After you've learned about the amazing personal stories and stories of success that surround Telekinesis, let's dig deeper in the ethics harnessing the power of thought over physical matter.

While you explore this intriguing field you should be aware of the impact on society that could be a result of telekinesis.

One of the most important ethical questions brought up by telekinesis concerns the power of control and authority. Given the capability to control objects using our brains, how can make sure that the capability is used in a responsible manner and to benefit the public good? Potential for abuse or manipulation is a serious concern because telekinetic capabilities are a possibility to exploit to gain personal advantage or in order to harm other people. It raises serious questions regarding individuals' autonomy, and the need for oversight and regulation.

Additionally, the emergence of telekinesis has far-reaching impacts on society. The old equilibrium of power and work may be altered and result in significant changes within various fields. If, for instance, the use of telekinesis is widespread the technology could make certain job positions obsolete, which could lead to an increase in unemployment and social inequality.

But there is the possibility of creating new industries and opportunities on telekinesis. This could alter the employment market.

Another ethical issue is the potential impact on private privacy. Telekinesis when not appropriately monitored or regulated, can possibly violate the privacy of individuals through permitting unauthorized access to their private spaces or belongings.

While we work to realize the power of telekinesis it is essential to look at this technology with a cautious eye taking into consideration the ethical implications as well as possible social impact. In addressing these concerns as well as establishing rules, we can make sure that this power the mind over matter is utilized with prudence and for the common benefit of society.

Pushing the Limits: Advanced Telekinetic Techniques

Learn how to take your telekinetic capabilities up a notch with the most advanced methods. Telekinesis is a field where it is never too late for improvement and growth. If you are able to master the latest techniques of telekinesis, you are able to test the limits of your skills and attain an increased level of control of your mind's ability to manage the flow of matter.

One of the most important elements of advanced telekinetic methods is mastering the art of telekinetic control. Focusing and concentration to an uncanny degree, which allows you to operate things with accuracy and elegance. By putting in a lot of practice and maintaining a determination, you'll be able to develop your brain to apply pressure on objects that have greater power and precision.

Another benefit of modern techniques for telekinetics is the expansion of the range of your telekinetic capabilities. When you've mastered the art of the art of controlling, you are able to play around with objects further than you are or that are larger. It is a must to have a thorough comprehension of the workings of telekinesis, as well as the capacity to harness the immense possibilities of the mind's capabilities.

Additionally, the most advanced techniques for telekinetics are about exploring the boundaries of your capabilities. In constant effort to push yourself beyond your expectations it is possible to discover incredible levels of telekinetic power. This could mean trying to simultaneously move several objects or even levitate larger objects or manipulating the objects in themselves.

It is essential to take on the latest telekinetic methods with an open-minded mind and an attitude of curiosity. Be open to the difficulties and setbacks as opportunities to grow and development. If you are committed and persistent you will discover the full potential of your telekinetic powers and be a master of your mind and the physical world.

Frequently Asked Questions

Telekinesis can be utilized to harm others?

Telekinesis is a real possibility to be employed for harmful reasons. The ethical implications of telekinesis is a complicated issue since it involves the capability to control physical objects using the ability of mind.

Telekinesis in popular culture is frequently presented as a powerful power which is able to be utilized in both good and bad. Although it can be used to be used for good purposes like helping with the rescue mission or helping with research in science but it is also employed to harm others, inflicting damage to other people or damaging property.

A responsible application of telekinesis is a careful assessment of implications and an enlightened moral guideline.

What can I do to protect my body from harm when I practice the art of telekinesis?

Do you feel a little sceptical regarding negative energy when you practice Telekinesis? Don't worry! We've got the best security techniques for energy specially for our readers.

The first step is to explore the connection between mind and body. When you establish a relationship between your mind and body via meditation as well as exercise that helps you ground, you build an insulator against negative thoughts.

Also, surrounded by positive environments and people will help to keep negative thoughts away.

Make sure you are protected. It is essential to have an enjoyable telekinetic experience!

Are there any risk or adverse effects that are associated with developing your telekinetic skills?

Telekinetic ability development can lead to possible implications for mental health. Be aware of the mental health effects that could arise like anxiety or stress.

In addition, ethical considerations must be considered while employing the power of telekinesis. There are many questions to be asked about how to use this ability and the possible negative effects it might cause other people.

It is essential to consider the process of developing telekinetic capabilities using a complete, logical mentality and think about the possible dangers and ethical implications.

Telekinesis can be taught to everyone or is it just available to a handful of individuals?

Telekinesis which is the capability to manipulate objects by using your mind, isn't just for a small group of people. Through the proper strategies and practices, everyone could develop this skill.

Beginning students can begin by focusing on their concentration and ability to visualize.

Many famous instances throughout the history of mankind including Nina Kulagina and Uri Geller prove that telekinesis can be a true phenomenon.

Although there are still doubters open-minded, an approach that is inclusive encourages exploration and development in this intriguing area.

Do you know of any study or proof of the possibility of Telekinesis?

Studies in science have investigated the possibility of telekinesis however, skeptics claim that there's no proof that supports the theory. Though some research studies have revealed fascinating results, they're generally criticized for the flaws in their methodology.

It is crucial to tackle this issue with a wide-ranging view and to continue researching the subject.

www.ingramcontent.com/pod-product-compliance
Lightning Source LLC
Chambersburg PA
CBHW070954080526
44587CB00015B/2310